Branch Lines of East

Volume C

Louth to Bardney

A. J. Ludlam

Published by the
Lincolnshire Wolds Railway Society

LWRS
PUBLICATIONS

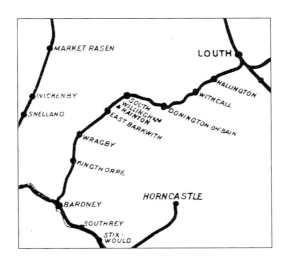

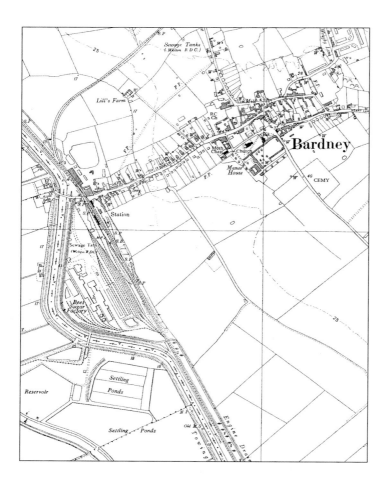

ISBN 978-0-9926762-5-4

The Lincolnshire Wolds Railway Society would like to thank Alf Ludlam and Phil Eldridge for giving their time to compile this publication, to Trevor Bateman, Michael Stewart and Leyland Penn for their contributions and to Allinson Print & Supplies for their support with the project.

Printed by Allinson Print & Supplies, Allinson House, Lincoln Way, Fairfield Industrial Estate, Louth, Lincolnshire LN11 0LS

Issue 1. February 2015.

CONTENTS

Bill Abbott in Hallington signal box in LNER days. Bill was "general factotum" at Hallington during World War 2.

Louth 13th June 1876

Sir

On behalf of the
Louth & Lincoln Railway Company
I hereby give notice that it is the
intention of the Company to open
their Railway constructed under
"the Louth & Lincoln Railway Act. 1866"
and "the Louth & Lincoln Railway Act. 1872"
and I shall be glad to receive
necessary forms

Your obt Sert
Fred. Sharpley

The Assistant Secretary
Railway Department
Board of Trade
Whitehall
London.

INTRODUCTION

This account of what was the most scenic branch line in Lincolnshire will concentrate on the Bardney end of the line. My reason for this is that I have covered activities at Louth in my previous book "Louth - a Lincolnshire Railway Centre".

The large village of Bardney stands on the banks of the River Witham, nine miles east of Lincoln. The river was an important trading route between Lincoln and the port of Boston from Roman times. A Benedictine abbey was founded at Bardney in the 7th century by King Ethelred of Mercia and his Queen, Ostryth, whose father - King Oswald of Northumbria, once lived at Bardney.

After the murder of Ostryth in 679 AD Ethelred renounced the crown and lived at Bardney until his death in 716 AD. It is believed that Queen Ostryth was buried in the abbey and Ethelred at King Hill, an ancient barrow in a field close by the route of the Louth to Bardney branchline. The Danes destroyed the abbey in 870 AD. A new one was built in 1087, the foundations of which are still visible.

A ferry was established across the River Witham at Bardney in 1714 and remained in use until 1893, when a bridge was erected at a cost of £7,250, to which the Great Northern Railway (GNR) contributed £3,000.

East Barkwith station, signal box and level crossing in **GNR** days, the staff look very smart, the stationmaster sporting a flower in his buttonhole.

Signalman Walter Prescott stands outside East Barkwith signal box. Note the brush and mop laid along the roof above his head.

LOUTH and BARDNEY.

Miles	Up.		Week Days only.				Miles	Down.		Week Days only.					
		mrn	mrn		aft	aft	aft			mrn	mrn		mrn		mrn	aft
—	**Louth** ....dep.	7 45	9 50	..	12 53	1 05	5 25	—	887 London (K. C.)...dep.	4 45	7 25	..	8 45	..	11 30	.. 3 0 ..
3	Hallington	..	10 2	..	..	3 16	5 26	—	887 Lincoln (L.N.E.) ,,	8 25	10 38	..	12 44	..	4 12	.. 6 30 ..
4¼	Withcall	7 54	10 7	..	..	3 21	6 3	—	Bardney ....dep.	8 45	11 28	..	4 32	..	6 55 ..
7¼	Donington-on-Bain....	8 3	10 16	..	12 53	3 30	6 12	4	Kingthorpe	8 52	..	1 25	..	4 39	.. 7 2 ..
10¼	South Willingham and	8 10	10 23	..	Bb 3 37	6 19	..	6	Wragby	8 53	11 39	..	1 31	..	4 45	.. 7 8 ..
12½	East Barkwith (Hainton	8 14	10 27	..	Bb 3 41	6 25	..	8¼	East Barkwith (Hainton	9 3	11 44	..	1 36	..	4 50	.. 7 13 ..
15¼	Wragby	8 20	10 33	..	12 43	3 47	6 29	10¼	South Willingham and	9 8	11 49	..	1 41	..	4 55	.. 7 18 ..
17¼	Kingthorpe	8 24	10 37	..	..	3 51	6 33	13¼	Donington-on-Bain	9 15	11 57	..	1 49	..	5 3	.. 7 25 ..
21¼	Bardney 887 ......arr.	8 31	10 44	..	12 57	3 58	6 40	16¼	Withcall	9 21	12 3	..	1 55	..	5 8	.. 7 31 ..
30¼	887 Lincoln (L. N. E.) arr.	9 0	11 4	..	1 24	4 17	7 7	18¼	Hallington	9 25	12 7	..	1 59	..	5 12	..
160¼	887 London (K. C.) ,,	..	3 47	..	4 20	9 12	..	21¼	Louth 888, 890 ......arr.	9 31	12 13	..	2 5	..	5 18	.. 7 40 ..

2

ARRIVAL OF THE RAILWAY

The first railway to arrive at Bardney was the Lincolnshire Loop line which ran from Peterborough to Bawtry, near Doncaster, via Spalding, Boston, Lincoln and Gainsborough. The line opened between Peterborough and Lincoln on 17th October, 1848, between Lincoln and Gainsborough on 9th April, 1849 and between there and Doncaster in July 1867.

Prior to the opening of the Louth & Lincoln Railway, Bardney was a through station, with up and down platforms, a station house of "Italianate" design, which was an architectural feature of the line, a goods shed and sidings completed the layout.

In 1866 the Louth & Lincoln Railway Company (L&LRC) made elaborate claims for freight traffic from the Nottinghamshire, Derbyshire and Erewash Valley coalfields. A mining engineer, Mr Roseby, estimated that there were 35,000,000 tons of good quality ironstone per square mile near Apley and 9,000,000 tons near Donington-on-Bain. There was talk of blast furnaces which would, if built, compete with any in the country in the manufacture of pig iron. The potential was

Very early days at Wragby station, the stationmaster and his family, the station staff and four platelayers make up the scene.

3

limitless, euphoria reigned supreme.

The GNR agreed to work the line for 50% of the takings. As well as local traffic, visitors from the Midlands, journeying to Cleethorpes, would be served by the branch. By using the new line a saving of three hours would be made over alternative routes via Boston or Lincoln, Market Rasen and Grimsby. No one seemed to question this doubtful claim that in order to save a few hours was a hope rather than a fact; and was just as strong an argument for the possible failure of the Louth and Lincoln should the agreement to divert traffic to the new line not be forthcoming.

The L&LRC was incorporated on 6th August 1866 with capital of £250,000 and Mortgage Debentures of £83,000. The original intention was for the branch to join the Loop line to the east of Five Mile House station. However, by April 1867 the Directors were reporting that problems over the purchase of land made it impossible to join the Loop at Five Mile House. Consultations with the GNR to find a solution were requested. After a long delay the Directors reported a disappointing local response to raising subscriptions. They unanimously agreed to ask the Board of Trade for permission to abandon the whole project. The application to wind up the company was made in 1870, but was refused.

Painters at the level-crossing at East Barkwith station in the early 20th century.

The next important meeting of the somewhat reluctant company was in April 1871 when it was decided to proceed with the project. An agreement with a Manchester civil engineer, Frederick Appleby was signed. The agreement gave the whole capital of the company and its borrowing powers to that gentleman. In return Mr Appleby was to be solely responsible for financing, purchasing, paying for and conveying land. The engineers Mr Myers and Mr Tolme were to construct the single line using 72 lb rail, and, in accordance with the 1866 agreement with the GNR, in which the GNR had agreed to operate the line, provided it was certified satisfactory by the Board of Trade upon completion. Instead of a junction at Five Mile House the branch would join the loop at Bardney, just north of the station. The junction here was reversed so all trains ran into a bay platform, access to the Loop being by means of crossovers only. This meant that trains from Louth would have to reverse here.

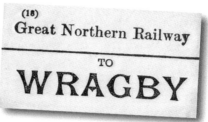

Construction began at the Louth end in January 1872, by July a 10 ft heading had been driven 90 yards at the eastern end and the same at the west end of Withcall tunnel. The tunnel was being driven through sandstone and chalk, considered favourable for tunneling. Shafts and headings had also begun on the shorter High Street tunnel, near South Willingham.

By the beginning of 1873 work had slowed down because of excessive rain saturating the ground and making carting impossible. However, the ten miles or so between Bardney and South Willingham were complete, work on the stations was progressing well and Withcall tunnel was within thirty yards of completion.

By August 1874 the tunnels were completed and track was being laid through them. High Street tunnel was 558 yards in length, the 971 yards of Withcall tunnel had caused many problems during its construction. Bad weather had continuously delayed work, the build-up of water being so great in October 1874, that it resulted in a deluge that washed men out of the tunnel. In November there was a strike by bricklayers, because their hands were so badly scalded by the wet lime that they could no longer hold their trowels. The death of Cornelius Janaway, in an accident involving a wagon in December was the culmination of the misfortunes relating to Withcall tunnel.

A goods train approaches South Willingham station from Louth at the turn of the century.

The short branch line platform at Bardney with station staff in attendance in GNR days. The 'Italianate' style of the station house is well seen as is the splendid station nameboard.

OPENING OF THE LINE

The opening of the branch proceeded as follows: the 10 miles 49 chains from Bardney to South Willingham, was opened to goods traffic on 9th November, 1874. This was extended a further 3 miles 5 chains to Donington-on-Bain by 27th September, 1875. The complete line was opened for goods traffic by 26th June, 1876.

Opening to passengers was delayed until 1st December, 1876, because Board of Trade Inspector, Captain Tyler, would not recommend its opening until turntables had been installed at Louth and Bardney.

A slight problem at Louth, in the form of the Louth Volunteer Corps rifle range, over which the line passed, briefly threatened the new passenger service. The GNR warned the Rifle Corps that they were not prepared to risk the lives of their passengers and that the service would be withdrawn unless that part of the line could be made safe. Such a guarantee was speedily forthcoming and the rifles were pointed in another direction.

The original passenger service consisted of five trains each way on weekdays only. This was reduced to four trains by January 1877, only a month after the services began. South Willingham station was renamed Hainton & South Willingham. A siding was opened at Withcall in July 1878, followed, a month later,

A busy scene at Wragby station in 1907, station staff assist passengers boarding the train bound for Louth.

by a small station, manned by a solitary stationmaster and a youthful porter in the "Agricultural Season".

The optimism engendered in the Prospectus was soon dispelled by early receipts, the 12 months July 1875 to June 1876 showed only £2,094 profits. The traffic from the Midlands did not materialize, the Nottingham and Grantham trains continued to work through Boston.

In June 1878 the L&LR Company appealed unsuccessfully to the GNR for financial assistance. Another approach was made after another bad year in 1880. In 1881 negotiations were re-opened, and, in August, the GNR expressed an interest in purchasing the branch for £200,000, this figure was slightly more than half the expenditure on the line. The L&LR was on the rack and it was a question of getting the best offer to cut their losses. Considering that traffic receipts between 1876 and 1881 had never produced enough money to pay the bank interest, it was no surprise the offer was unanimously accepted by an Extraordinary Meeting of shareholders on 20th December, 1881.

Royal Assent was given for the transfer and the L&LR Company passed into the possession of the GNR on 30th June, 1881, an ignoble end to a bold but foolhardy piece of railway speculation.

The track curves away under the road bridge at Donington-on-Bain station. Stationmaster Margisson and the Reverend Jollye of Withcall stand in the foreground.

Lincoln-based Stirling 0-4-2 No 577A with a passenger train at Hainton and South Willingham station in 1920.

Hallington signal box in Great Northern days, including the signalman and platelaying gang which was based at nearby Withcall station. *Peter Chapman Collection.*

Hallington station with its row of fire buckets and a delightful child's dolls pram. Stationmaster William Pickering, an unknown member of staff, and signalman E. Hickling in their GNR uniforms stand on the platform.

Bardney signal box in August 1970, with a selection of road transport available. The box with its attractive decorative bargeboards looks its age, but the steps are new. Morrell's canning factory is behind the box. *P. Grey.*

BARDNEY JUNCTION

The original intention was for the L&LR branch to join the Boston-Lincoln line at Five Mile House station, with a junction facing Lincoln. However, land purchases proved problematic and the branch opened with a junction at Bardney facing the wrong way for trains to Lincoln. A new signal box and a double line junction was installed at Bardney. The final arrangement was of three platforms, two of which formed an island with a canopied waiting shelter, the third was a short platform alongside the station buildings, used by the Louth trains.

A second signal box was opened at Bardney in conjunction with the opening of the branch. The signal boxes were known as Bardney North and Bardney South, the latter was situated east of the platforms and adjacent to the goods yard. North box was next to the level crossing at the north end of the station. North box worked the South box's down and up home signals during the times when the latter was closed. After the closure of South box in 1924, North box assumed the title "station box" and received a new frame along the back wall. Bardney was a three-shift signal box, dealing with traffic on the Loop, as well as trains from Louth and those visiting the sugar factory and Morrell's siding.

The splendid running-in boards on the island platform at **Bardney** in June 1951. *M. Black.*

With a round of coal applied to the firebox class C12 4-4-2T No 67379 waits at the short branch line platform at Bardney, with a passenger train for Louth in May 1951. *M. Black.*

Lincoln-based class A5 4-6-2T No 69804 shunts the yard at Bardney while working a pick-up goods on 28th April, 1954. 69804 was built for the GCR in 1911 and withdrawn in April 1958. *H. C. Casserley.*

After running their engine round the train, the footplate crew, driver Bill Cartwright and Fireman Fred Hardy, take a breather before returning to Louth aboard class C12 4-4-2T No 67352 on 14th June, 1951. *C. Bayes.*

Bardney station looking towards Boston in 1930 with some nice incidental details, such as the platelayer's trolley and the milk churns, standing near the station buildings. The line running from the sugar factory runs off to the right beyond the water column. *D. Thompson.*

Class J11 0-6-0 passes the impressive stationmaster's house and enters Bardney station with a pick-up goods train off the Louth-Bardney branch on 13th October 1951, less than a month before closure to passenger traffic. *P. H. Wells.*

The island platform at Bardney with its canopied waiting shelter. Branch line stock stands in the platform used by trains from Louth.

Guard Froggatt unlocks and opens the crossing gates at Bardney, while class 08 No 08101 waits to take a delivery of coal for the sugar factory into the station area on 23rd May, 1980. This is also a good view of the, by this time, disused Morrell's canning factory siding and canopy. *M. Roughley.*

MORRELL'S CANNING FACTORY

The factory stood alongside the Loop line, immediately north of the level crossing next to the station. Access to its siding was from the Louth branch. The siding usually held eighteen vanfits and a couple of mineral wagons for coal delivery. There were seven positions for unloading empty cans which were sent from the Metal Box Company of Worcester, these came in "shockfits".

To make it easy for positioning, eleven empty vanfits were shunted in and these were used for loading, as required, by the factory. Two shunts were completed each day, at 12 noon and at 6.00 pm. The mid-day shunt was the most critical as it had to fit into the factory lunch time. It was mostly a case of replacing the empty can vans for the afternoon work. The evening shunt included the loaded wagons of canned vegetables and dog food.

There were two places between the vanfits under the loading canopy and the coal hopper. When there were two coal wagons in the siding the empty wagon was pinched along to allow the second wagon access to the hopper. These wagons were emptied by hand. To gain some idea of the importance of the mid-day shunt, on occasions a British Railways "Britannia" Pacific locomotive, running light engine from New England to Immingham, was diverted to do the work. No 70012 "John of Gaunt" was seen on such duties. The route availability of the siding was Group 8.

For safety reasons a key was obtained from the signalman, subject to the Louth branch being clear. The key was inserted into a box and turned, thus activating the bell system, which warned everyone that a shunt was about to take place. The shunter walked along the gantry to check the van doors and that factory staff was clear of the siding. He then made his way to the ground frame and inserted another key to activate the points to the siding. After the shunt the procedure was reversed.

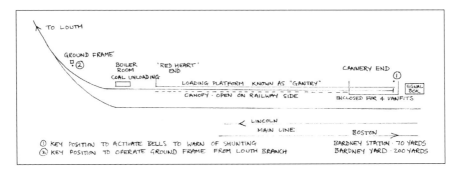

Two photos of driver Albert Burns of Louth, wearing his driver's "uniform" and in civies at his retirement.

The sugar factory at Bardney opened for business in 1927, and this view of the factory shows clearly some of the lines that went into the site from the main line through Bardney. We see here the river passing round the factory site, and the carbonisation plant in the foreground, with a rail-mounted crane at work.

Tunnel Vision

Winding its way through the Lincolnshire Wolds, the Louth-Bardney line boasted two tunnels.

The 558-yard long South Willingham (High Street) tunnel is pictured above in 1982. A major landslip occured near the mouth of the eastern end on 21st July, 1939.

Pictured on the right is the 971 yard long Withcall tunnel.

Bardney Junction

Bardney station looking west in September 1967. The short branch line platform previously used by the Louth trains can be seen on the right.

The elegant lines of Bardney station in July 1982. The area of lighter coloured bricks to the right indicates where the station nameboard was located. Coal was still being delivered to the sugar factory at this time.

By January 1976 items of railway infrastructure have started to disappear including the signal box, semaphore signals and telegraph poles. *A. Young.*

Looking north from Bardney station in September 1970. Morrell's canning factory with its long loading dock can be seen on the far side of the level crossing. *B. Cable.*

Above: The tracks may have gone but Donington-on-Bain, like many other stations on the line, is still with us.

Left: An LNER examination form issued for C12 4-4-2T No 67384 at Louth shed in December 1949. *L. Penn.*

Below: 67384 carrying its 1925 number 4531, seen here at Grantham shed. It worked at Louth from August 1949 until withdrawal in 1956.

THE SUGAR FACTORY

In Britain it was a long time before we recognised the advantages of sugar beet cultivation. At the outbreak of World War 1 there was only one sugar factory in England, at Cantley in Norfolk, which opened in 1912. During the war we recognised the danger of our reliance upon foreign sources for sugar. Partly for this reason and partly for the benefits that would accrue to agriculture, it was determined to establish a home-grown sugar industry. The Sugar Beet Subsidy Act of 1925 encouraged investment enabling eighteen factories to be built.

In 1925 Henry Beacon held a series of meetings in local towns and villages announcing the building of a sugar factory at Bardney. By the time the factory opened in September 1927 he had 11,255 acres of sugar beet under cultivation. This produced a crop of 81,380 tons of sugar beet which made 10,085 tons of sugar, 6,111 tons of animal feed and 980 tons of molasses.

Most farmers grew sugar beet because it left them with a fair profit and provided valuable by products for feeding stock in the form of beet tops and pulp. The crop fitted well into the annual routine and gave work to the farm labourers following the corn and potato harvests.

The entrance to the Bardney sugar factory sidings was off the Loop line, about half-a-mile south of Bardney station on the down side. A trailing connection operated by

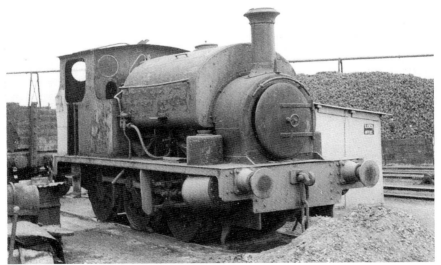

Hudswell Clarke 0-6-0ST No 1604 at the Bardney sugar factory in April 1974. *H. A. Gamble.*

25

ground frame, led into extensive sidings which occupied some eight roads, with a spur which ran to various points in the factory system. The sidings formed a continuous run-round emerging as a single line back to the station to rejoin the main line.

The factory had its own shunting engine, Hudswell Clarke 0-6-0ST No 1604. It was delivered sporting Midland Railway red livery on 15th August, 1928. It was taken out of service in 1970 and sold to the Nene Valley Railway in 1979. At present it is based on the Mid-Suffolk Light Railway at Brockford station, Wetheringsett, awaiting restoration. An 0-4-0 diesel engine No 327974, built by Ruston of Lincoln, was purchased in 1954 and worked at the factory until the internal system was closed and the track lifted in 1983.

Coal for the factory was brought from Holmes Yard in Lincoln by the Bardney pilot, which arrived at about 11.00 am. It was left at the south end of the factory sidings. Motive power was usually a class J6 or J11 0-6-0 - later a BR Standard 4MT from Lincoln shed. The load was often twenty wagons of washed singles in 16 ton mineral wagons from Blidworth Colliery.

The last part of the Boston to Lincoln line to survive was the nine miles between Lincoln and Bardney. It was singled and effectively became a branch serving the sugar factory. During the close season, from February to October, coal was delivered to the factory and stockpiled in readiness for the season. This arrangement remained in place until the closure of the line, which was lifted in 1983. The sugar factory closed in 2001, all processing staff leaving the site on 9th February.

An aerial view of Bardney station and the sugar factory, in 1927. The Boston-Lincoln line runs diagonally across the photo with Bardney station in the right-hand corner.

THE NOCTON LIGHT RAILWAY

On the opposite side of the River Witham to the sugar factory was the Nocton Estate, which was established by W. Dennis & Sons in 1919. It operated the longest agricultural narrow gauge railway in Lincolnshire. Sugar beet from the estate was delivered to sidings on the river bank where wagons were unloaded into the "Dennis Bunker". The beet was transferred to the factory by a mechanical grab, running along a gantry across the river.

The Nocton Estate covered 8,000 acres. The idea for the 1ft 11¹/₂ in gauge railway was inspired by the estate manager Major Webber, who has seen, first hand, how effective narrow gauge railways were in the terrible conditions of World War 1. He purchased great quantities of narrow gauge track and rolling stock from the Army Surplus depot at Arras, in France. The railway eventually reached 23 miles in length and was used to move potatoes, sugar beet and grain.

The Nocton Estate's Simplex locomotive, together with two narrow-gauge wagons, stands alongside a British Railways box van in Smith's standard-gauge siding. The narrow-gauge wagons were converted to carry fuel for tractors. *Stewart Squires Collection.*

Class J6 0-6-0 No 64219 of Lincoln shed with a pick-up goods at Wragby station in 1959. *M. Black.*

Wragby station from the level crossing in 1953. This was the only station on the branch with two platforms. The Player's cigarette advert proclaiming, "The choice of a lifetime" has a certain irony about it. *P. Sutton.*

A Journey over the Branch

W. McGowan Gradon described a journey over the branch in 1945.

"Cutting through the southern end of the Lincolnshire Wolds, this picturesque branch, 21 miles in length, has several unusual features to commend it to the railway enthusiast. The scenery is delightful and in complete contrast to the flatness usually associated with the greater part of the county.

The branch leaves the main line just west of Bardney station, and curves away sharply to the north. Kingthorpe, the first station, 4 miles from Bardney, has a goods loop and a single platform. Wragby, the principal station on the line, and the only one boasting two platforms and a passing loop for passenger trains, is 2 miles beyond Kingthorpe. It has a fair-sized goods yard which handles a considerable amount of agricultural traffic. So far the line has passed through fairly level agricultural country, which continues another 3 miles to East Barkwith, where the southern edge of the Wolds can be seen.

After a short sharp fall into East Barkwith station, which has a single platform

Kingthorpe station, with its single siding line June 1951. The bridge takes the **B1202 Bardney** to **Wragby** road over the line, whereas all the other brick-built buildings along the line survive, nothing remains of Kingthorpe. *M. Black.*

and a goods loop, the line begins to climb towards the Wolds and gradients steepen to more than 1 in 70. Curving north-eastwards the track reaches South Willingham, 1¾ miles from East Barkwith. Here there is the usual single platform, a goods loop and a short siding beyond the station. The line now turns almost due east, and, passing through a cutting in the folds of the hills, enters High Street tunnel. Emerging from the tunnel the line drops sharply down a valley between the hills to Donington-on-Bain, 3 miles from South Willingham. Donington is a staff station and there is a goods yard a similar size to the one at Wragby. Although trains can be crossed here, the loop is not normally used and the station has only one platform. Immediately beyond Donington the line starts to climb steeply, reaching a maximum gradient of 1 in 65. The summit is reached in the middle of Withcall tunnel, which carries the line through the last shoulder of the Wolds down to Withcall, 3 miles from Donington, the railway is carried on a series of embankments and round a number of sharp reverse curves, one which has a long length of check rail. Withcall

station stands on a gradient of 1 in 79 falling towards Louth. From here the line gradually levels out into gently undulating farming country. Hallington, 1¾ miles from Withcall, has a similar layout to East Barkwith. Finally the line curves round to the north and joins the Boston to Grimsby main line less than half a mile from Louth station, where there is a short bay platform on the up side to accommodate branch trains.

Except at Wragby, all home and starting signals have the up and down arms mounted on the same posts. Several of these have the lamps and spectacles placed much lower than the signal arms. At South Willingham the signals are left in the "off" position, except when there is shunting taking place. Level crossing at stations which are not block posts prevent this practice. A trip from Bardney to Louth on the footplate of class C12 No 4501 was an interesting experience. The train consisted of two close-coupled ex-GNR articulated coaches and an ex-North British eightwheeler, built at Cowlairs in 1901. Although the train was of modest weight, the gradients made it quite a stiff task for the little 45 year old engine. After the fire was made up at Bardney it was necessary to replenish it only three times, at Wragby, approaching High Street tunnel, and at Donington-on-Bain. Steam pressure never fell below 155 Ib and on the down gradients some quite brisk running was done, with speeds of around 45 mph."

Withcall station and signal box looking down the incline to Hallington in August 1953.

Class C12 4-4-2T No 67384 of Louth shed stands at Donington-on-Bain station with a passenger train from Louth to Bardney in April 1951. *M. Black.*

Hainton and South Willingham station seen from the signal box, looking west, in June 1951. *M. Black.*

Donington-on-Bain station seen from the road bridge, looking west, in April 1951. The signal box in the distance stands near the throat of the goods yard, which was situated behind the station buildings. *C. Bremner-Smith.*

Class J6 0-6-0 No 64219 runs over the stream and passes Kingthorpe station with a brake van on a pick-up goods in October 1959. Built in 1913 for the GNR, No 64219 was a Lincoln-based engine from 1958 to 1960 and withdrawn in November 1961. *M. Black.*

Class C12 4-4-2T No 67379 with ex-GCR Suburban coach No 5258, stands at Kingthorpe station with the 3.57 pm passenger train from Louth to Bardney, in June. 1951. *M. Black.*

Class C12 4-4-2T No 67364 stands in the bay platform at Louth with a passenger train for Bardney, in May 1950. The engine shed is seen behind the train. Although No 67364 has a Louth 40C shed plate on its smokebox door it has "Immingham" inscribed on its buffer beam. *M. Black.*

Steam everywhere as class C12 4-4-2T No 67384 approaches Donington-on-Bain station, with a passenger train from Louth, in April, 1951. Note the signal low down on the post so that it could be seen through the road over-bridge to the east of the station. *M. Black.*

Class C12 4-4-2T No 67384 stands in Withcall station, with a Barney bound passenger train, in April 1951. It has had a stiff climb through Hallington station to Withcall and will continue to climb until the middle of Withcall tunnel. *M. Black.*

HALLINGTON

Marshal Dale was a farmer, a user of the line and an outspoken critic of its closure. "Being the son of a farmer with a well-established large farm in the Binbrook area of Lincolnshire, I was somewhat surprised when my father announced that he had taken a farm near Louth, with a railway running right by it. This was in 1940 at the outset of World War 2. The Ministry of Agriculture were telling farmers to grow certain crops which were in short supply at the time. Father decided that a move close to the railway would make his sugar beet crop more profitable as it cost only 4/6d a ton delivered to Bardney by rail, compared to 6/- by road.

Apart from the sugar beet, the line was little used by us at this time. I do, however, remember having a Lincoln Red bull I had purchased at Lincoln Fair sent to Hallington by rail. Later, in 1947 when we decided to plant strawberry and gooseberry crops, most of the produce was put on the train at Hallington, to be taken to Boston and Wisbech. Here the main sales took place, the crop being bought for canning or jam making.

I got to know the last stationmaster at Hallington, Bob Cox, very well. Bob kept

Hallington station looking east in April 1951. The wall clock and its canopy is well seen. *M. Black.*

his garden alongside the line immaculate, having plenty of time to do so with only two or three trains a day. A predecessor of Bob's at Hallington used to get himself into hot water with repeated regularity. The problem was his inability to rise in the mornings in time to unlock the crossing gates. Drivers used to like to keep a good turn of speed to cope with the steep incline to Withcall. Being stopped at Hallington gates resulted in the morning air being assailed by language which was quite unrepeatable.

Another good friend was the Reverend Wyer-Honey, of Raithby, who used the line to transport two or three of his hunting horses to meets at Hainton, Wragby and Willingham, as well as the Burton Hunt near Lincoln. Of course he would try to encourage the huntsmen to arrange the final run of the day in the direction of the Louth area, thus saving himself a long hack back. The good clergyman's Daily Telegraph and Times newspapers would be collected from Hallington station at 8.20 am.

The threat of closure made all of us concerned as to the effect such an act would have on us personally. As well as transport for my sugar beet and fruit crops, the passing trains, in liaison with my tummy, usually reminded me of when mealtimes were due."

Hallington signal box and the siding with a novel end, in April 1951. The steady climb from Louth can be seen. *M. Black.*

World War II

During World War II, 233 Maintenance Unit had several railheads at stations along the branch. These were used to supply armaments to the aerodromes of "Bomber County", Wragby, South Willingham, Donington-on-Bain and Withcall were used for this purpose. Hallington was used as an empties dump. From here empty cases would be returned to the munitions factories.

233 Maintenance Unit had a bomb dump on the old Roman road between Caistor and Horncastle. Known as "Bomb Alley", it was guarded by soldiers with fixed bayonets stationed at every road junction. Thousand of bombs destined for Germany were stacked on grass verges as far as the eye could see.

Most of the bombs delivered by rail came via Donington-on-Bain, which perfectly suited this kind of traffic due to its position in a valley between two long tunnels. A quiet little wayside station, well equipped with sidings. Mr Jones, the stationmaster at Donington-on-Bain, said they often had two special bomb trains arrive at the station during a day and sometimes more. "There was a time when our yard and every other on the line was filled with bombs - we had thousands upon thousands of them".

The fireman puts a round of coal into the firebox before class N5 0-6-2T No 69306 tackles the I in 79 climb to the centre of Withcall tunnel with a passenger train from Louth in April 1951. No doubt he was not the most popular person with the lady with the washing on the line. *M. Black.*

The last train enters Wragby station on a wet day, 1st February, 1960 watched by a group of local "spotters". Lincoln-based class A5 4-6-2T No 69808 was one of the last three of the class to be withdrawn, in November 1960. *R. Bones.*

THE 1946 EXPLOSION

Ex-GNR class D3 No 4317, with driver Jack Ingamells, fireman Geoff Jackson and guard Arthur Dodman, was returning morning goods from Bardney to Louth. It was working hard out of South Willingham on the climb to High Street tunnel when a hot ember from the engine's chimney landed in a wagon part-way along the train containing propane cylinders packed in straw. The straw ignited and was burning fiercely by the time the fire was noticed about a quarter of a mile from Donington-on-Bain. Geoff Jackson and Arthur Dodman isolated the burning wagon by detaching behind and drawing forward, uncoupling the blazing wagon and drawing forward again. The intense heat caused burns to the fireman and guard. By this time cylinder tops were being blown 200-300 yards. Before fireman Jackson could get clear the cylinders exploded peppering his overalls with holes, like those made by shot blast. The explosion caused the blazing vehicle to run back onto the rear portion of the train setting fire to several coal wagons.

The local fire brigade attended to the fire and an ambulance came to administer first aid. Geoff Jackson's burns caused him to be in bandages to his hands, face and legs for six weeks.

For their bravery the three members of the crew were awarded the LNER Medal, in recognition of courage and resource. It was presented to them at Kings Cross by Sir Ronald Matthews, Chairman of the LNER.

Class J11 0-6-0 approaches Donington-on-Bain signal box with a passenger train from Bardney to Louth in 1939. The entrance to the goods yard can be seen to the right of the engine. *B. Abbott.*

Linesman Tom Eyre, with an unknown employee and his wife, outside the signal box at Withcall station in July 1939. The odd-shaped brush held by the man in uniform was used to whitewash the edge of the platform. *B. Abbott.*

The isolated location of Kingthorpe station is well shown in this August 1953 photo. The road from Bardney to Wragby can be briefly seen behind the tree on the left, the station was connected to the road by the track running off to the left. *D. Thompson.*

Runaway Train

Stan Fanthorpe recalled a near disaster on the line in 1944. He was fireman to driver Priestly of Lincoln. The train was in the charge of guard Sellars and consisted of 18 wagons, destined for various stations along the line. Every wagon contained one large bomb. The first station at which wagons were detached was South Willingham. The engine went forward with five wagons leaving the rest and the brake van on the single line, the engine coupled up to five empty wagons in the siding, with the intention of backing them onto the rest of the train. However, all that could be seen was the rest of the train disappearing down the incline in the direction of East Barkwith.

The train ran through East Barkwith station and demolished the crossing gates. Fortunately communication was established with the signal man at Wragby who was able to open the gates. He estimated the speed of the wagons at 40 mph as they passed through the station. The train finally came to a rest in Kingthorpe Bottom, see-sawing itself to a standstill. The train crew at Willingham feared that the wagons might collide with the Lincoln-Louth pick-up goods, due on the branch at that time. Fortunately it was still at Bardney.

Guard Sellars was held responsible for not securing the brakes on the train. Because of wartime restrictions on reporting the movement of armaments the incident wasn't reported in the press.

World War 1 saw the felling of many pine trees around Withcall which were taken by rail for use shoring up trenches on the battlefields of France and Belgium. After the almost total deforestation of Wales the Government began to turn to places like Withcall for trench props.

An embankment near Withcall was covered with white violets, reputedly the largest plot in Britain. Quite a trade built-up between Withcall and the London flower markets. The London purchasers would send containers and white ribbon every year. Children would gather the flowers and tie them into bunches, and pack them into the moss filled containers ready for the journey to London. As much as 5/- could be made during the three week season. The violet money would often be used by mothers to buy children's clothes.

Class C12 4-4-2T running down the 1 in 79 gradient into Withcall station with a passenger train from Bardney to Louth in April 1951. In the 1920s a staff of seven were based at Withcall, a stationmaster, signalman, porter and four platelayers. *M. Black.*

Class N5 0-6-2T No 69306 of Louth shed stands at the south end of Louth station with a passenger train for Bardney in June 1951. Louth South signal box can be glimpsed behind the telegraph pole, so to the overall station roof and the engine shed. *M. Black.*

CLOSURE

The letter from British Railways announcing plans to close the branch to all traffic was read to members of the Louth RDC at a meeting in March 1951. After a protracted discussion the Councillors agreed with BR's proposal to close the line to passengers, but opposed its closure to freight traffic. They felt it was essential that the line be maintained for the delivery of goods and the collection of produce from the farms in that part of the Wolds.

BR decide that the last passenger train over the branch would be the 3.57 pm on Saturday, 3rd November. Freight traffic would continue on the line for the foreseeable future.

On the appointed day the designated engine was, appropriately, class C12 4-4-2T No 67379, the driver Bill "Bumper" Cartwright, of Tennyson Road, Louth, firemen Fred Hardy of St Bernards Avenue and guard Cyril Thompson of Linden Walk. Because the usual Louth to Bardney rolling stock was somewhat antiquated, it was, for the comfort of passengers on the last trip, replaced by coaches borrowed from the Mablethorpe branch, numbers E86048 and E82861.

The last passenger train at Bardney on 3rd November, 1951. Class C12 4-4-2T No 67379, with a wreath on its smokebox door, is surrounded by its crew, driver Bill "Bumper" Cartwright, fireman Fred Hardy, guard Cyril Thompson, the Bardney stationmaster and staff.

Another C12 was cleaned and standing by in Louth yard in case there was sufficient demand to fill more carriages, in which case 67352 would have double-headed with 67379 - what a finale that would have been!

The journey from Louth began at 3.57 pm with about 50 passengers on board. At Bardney the return journey began in heavy rain. A considerable crowd had gathered at Louth station for the arrival of the 7.21 pm from Bardney. The train arrived dead on time. People gathered round the engine intent upon getting the autographs of the crew.

The final passenger journey between Louth and Bardney meant a number of staff at Louth shed (40C) became redundant. These included three drivers, six firemen and six other grades, including cleaners.

After closure to passengers the line continued a goods only service until 1956, when, on 17th September, the section between Louth and Donington-on-Bain was closed. The 1st December, 1958 saw the section between Donington and Wragby succumb. And finally the Wragby to Bardney section was closed on 1st February, 1960, 86 years after the L&LR opened the same section in 1874.

Most of the trackbed still exists, much of it used as farm tracks. All of the station buildings survive, except those at Kingthorpe and Withcall. It was suggested that perhaps the dmu could have saved the line, but they were used on the Louth to Mablethorpe branch, which had always been a better financial proposition compared with the Louth to Bardney, it too closed in the 1960s. Its only salvation would have been as a preserved line, a great opportunity missed.

Class J11 0-6-0 No 64320, of Louth shed, shunts the yard at Wragby on 25th July, 1952. A box of pigeons and an empty sleeper wagon were collected from here. *J. Cupit.*

Hainton and South Willingham station and signal box look unkempt, the garden overgrown, in this August 1953 view. The closure to passengers two years earlier is evidenced by the lack of white edging to the platform. *D. Thompson.*

On 16 May 1954 the RCTS operated a 'Lincolnshire Railtour' which started from Nottingham (Midland) station, then worked to Lincoln with LMS 4-4-0 Compound No 40935, where the train changed to former GNR motive power using 'J6' 0-6-0 No 64199 to travel over the Bardney to Louth line. The special is pictured here pausing at Donington-on-Bain. *H. Ballantyne.*

The track at Wragby station is overgrown, piled up sleepers in the goods yard and track lifting cranes, all add to this depressing scene in June 1961, after closure of the branch. *M. Black.*

Tracklifting taking place on the Bardney line in June 1961. *M. Black.*